ELEVEN LETTERS & OTHER WRITINGS

John Argyropoulos

Translated by: D.P. Curtin

ELEVEN LETTERS & OTHER WRITINGS

Copyright @ 2024 Dalcassian Press

All rights reserved. No part of this publication may be reproduced, distributed, or transmitted in any form or by any means, including photocopying, recording, or other electronic or mechanical methods, without the prior written permission of the publisher, except in the case of brief quotations embodied in critical reviews and certain other non-commercial uses permitted by copyright law. For permission request, write to Dalcassian Press at dalcassianpublishing at gmail.com

ISBN: 979-8-3302-2584-2 (Paperback)

Library of Congress Control Number:
Author: Curtin, D.P. (1985-)

Printed by Ingram Content Group, 1 Ingram Blvd, La Vergne, Tennessee

First printing edition 2024.

ELEVEN LETTERS & OTHER WRITINGS

A COMPENDIUM

OF THE RULES AND FORMS OF REASONING BY JOHN ARGYROPULUS

EXTRACTED FROM ALL THE RULES AND COMPOUNDED BY THE GRACE OF PHILIP VALORIUS, HIS DISCIPLE.

Of the universals

Universal or predicable non-transcendent are five Genus, Difference, Species, Proper and Incident. Genus is that which is predicated of several different species, this very thing. Genus is another very general thing, which indeed is only a genus, and is never a species; for the reason that it has no other thing above itself that can be used as a genus, such as substance, quality, and the like, something subordinate, which indeed is both genus and species. Species to the highest, genus to the underworld, such as animals, scientists and the like.

A species is that which is submitted to a genus, or that which is predicated of individuals without any middle ground. Another species is very special: which, indeed, is only a species, as Man, Horse. Albedo, and whatever is of this kind, is another subaltern, which indeed is both species and genus; likewise, the subordinate kind, such as a conscious animal, color, and whatever is similar.

The difference is that by which one thing differs from another, or by which a species exceeds the genus, or that which is the same in essence, of which it is said to be predicated. Some of the differences are separable, such as walking, sleep, and the like; others are inseparable, such as walking, sleep, and the like; some are inseparable, to which the one is accidental, such as the blackness of Ethiopia and the whiteness of the cherry tree, and the other by itself, which indeed alone is divided into genera. and the constitutive of species, by which reason and specific are called, as rational and irrational; that of a man, that of a beast, such is the difference.

That which consists of something universal or happens by itself is proper. It is indeed said that the proper use of another thing happens to someone alone, but it does not belong to anyone of those who are under him, such as to heal, with respect to man, and to play the lyre. Something else happens to someone and belongs to each of those who are placed under him. However, it does not happen to him alone, as bipeds and quadrupeds. For that belongs to a man, this belongs to a lion: this is proper. Another thing happens only to such a person, and it belongs to all that are under him, and it always belongs to him. This is properly said to be proper, and it receives a mutual predication with the one to whom it belongs. For whatever is man is laughable, and whatever is laughable is man.

Accidents are those which can be present and absent without the corruption of the subject, and that which can be present and not present in the same subject. This is twofold. For one thing is separable, as sleep, walking, and the like; another is inseparable, as whiteness with respect to cherry, and blackness with respect to corm, and Ethiopic, and pitch. This can be done by free thought without corrupting the subject.

Of Predications

There is a predicament between the concepts of the superior and the infernal, in which the predicates of the superior are subjected to the force of the subordinate nature of the infernal. The predicates in which there are those which we have said are ten predicables, substance, quality, quality, to someone or relation, where, when, to have, to be situated, to act, to suffer. To which of course every non-transcendent substance, such as a man, an ox, a horse, is reduced to the concept; quantity, as number, line, surface, quality, as warmth, whiteness, sweetness, bitterness; relation, such as paternity, sonship, similarity and dissimilarity: where, as in the forum, in the temple, in Florence, Rome; when, as to-day, to-morrow, to-day, to-day, to-day, and whatever is like these;

to have, to be clothed, armed, and the like; to be in position, to lie down, to stand, and to sit; to act, to cut, burn, prick, and kill; to suffer, to be cut, burned, pierced, and beaten. And since each of these is indeed conceived or said by itself, there is absolutely no affirmation or negation from it; but when they are connected with each other, the affirmation or the negation continually flourishes.

Of Substance

Of substance the body is one thing, and the bodies are another; the body is one thing animate, another inanimate; Animate is one thing of the sensitive, another of the non-sensuous; Of the senses, which is indeed an animal, another is participles, and another is an exponent of reason; the partaker of strength is one mortal, another immortal. There is man, under whom are individual men, as Cicero, Scipio, Plato, here is heaven, under which and in like manner this heaven is, and the parts of it undergoing similar conditions. But the exponent of reason is the beast, under which the different species of many animals are individually placed by their differences, just as man is placed under each of which individuals differ only in number, under which horse this horse and that, under these oxen and that ox, and in the same way in the rest. In the same way the non-sensuous itself must be divided, which indeed is evidently flat, which is diffused by difference into the grass, the bush, and the tree; and indeed, the genus veluti is divided into various species, into the malua, the marubim, the verarum, and the like. But if these are the most special kinds, under them the particulars are placed, under the bad this and that, under the bad this and that, and in the same way with the rest. Now the bush is divided into the bush, the rose, and such species by differences, which, if they are most special, the individuals are placed under them in succession, under the bush this and that, under the rose this and that, and in a similar manner with the rest. Trees are also used as a genus, and it is itself divided into species by differences, into the walnut, the fig, the olive, the pine, the fir, and other similar genera, under which they are most specialized, the fig tree and the rest in the same way. The same is to be done in the animation. For it is also divided as a genus by its differences into species, into elements, in which are fire, air, water, earth, and those which are composed of the elements. , sulfur: that kind and whatever falls between these and the elements. Finally, the substance experienced by the body is very similar in all respects. For it is to be divided by differences such as the genus, and it is divided into its own species. It is evident that there are these separate substances, which we are wont to call minds and intelligences, in which and in each species the individual is eternally one. Let the glorious God be welcomed, who is indeed unlimited and infinite, and by this agreement the predicament of substance can be more fully divided. But Aristotle seems to have distributed it in this way. He says that substance is not another first, another second through the first of any individual; by understanding the second species and genera; and indeed, this he asserts to be the first and most proper and greatest of substances. But he says that species and genera are not so much substances as species, but rather substances than genera.

Not to be contended with every substance in the subject, and if not alone, for substance also belongs to difference. It behooves the first substance to signify something: it also behooves every substance not to be contrary to itself, and not to receive within itself degrees of greater or lesser substance through latitude. However, it seems to be most immediate in substance that one and the same thing should persist, and that it should be receptive to its opposites by its change. And these are enough of the things said.

TO NICODEMOS TRAGKEDINAN

From Florence, 1 Aug. 1460

Johannes Argyropolus of Constantinople to Nicodemus, the most noble and distinguished man, Lord Nicodemus, the most serene duke of Milan, the excellent orator, greeting his father.

I did not feel your withdrawal. For if I had felt and asked your favor to carry out that matter and had given a letter to the Most Serene Prince. Now at last I felt it, and at once wrote these letters to your service, and sent them to the most serene. I beseech your kindness to do the matter more diligently, to give my letters to the most serene, and to recommend me strongly to your serenity. For I am his faithful and perpetual servant. Farewell, dear husband, and love me. From Florence 1 Aug. 1460

The boy whom we have spoken of, Theodore, he is called Rhaul, and is the son of a noble man, Nicholas Rhaul, a most noble and magnificent man. I saw and understood what your nobility wrote to me, and also what the most illustrious and eloquent man Philelphus understood. And since I do not have that book of Plutarch at home, I will make an effort to have it a little later, and to see the passage in which it stands; then I will write at your service.

TO THE SAME

From Florence, Sept. 5, 1460

Johannes Argyopolus of Constantinople greeting the most noble and distinguished man, Lord Nicodemus, his beloved.

And a little while ago I gave a letter to your lordship together with the letter, I gave to him, and I do the same now and again. I beg you, therefore, to give these letters also to the Most Serene Prince, and to commend me to him highly, and also that boy of whom I have spoken to your nobility, who indeed lives under the guardianship of the most illustrious prince, and is called Rhaul, the son of a noble Greek man, Lord Nicholas Rhaulis Issis. But if what I said to your nobility has been obtained, let me know beforehand by letter. If less be done, nevertheless, I beseech your highness to commend the aforesaid child to my most serene prince. I am more bound to render this service to your highness than the rest. Good luck, and make sure that we have a letter from the Most Serene Prince for what we have written, so that we can obtain some authority by interceding with you at all. Goodbye again, with happiness and love from me as usual. From Florence on September 5, 1460.

TO THE DUKE OF MILAN

FRANCIS SFORZA

From Florence Sept. 5, 1468

Most illustrious and Most Serene Prince. A little while ago I gave a letter to your Most Illustrious Lordship through the noble Man Noxious. And now I am also writing. This, indeed, is not, as I think, an intrusive man, but will be seen as strongly obliged. For what else should benevolent absent servants do towards their masters, then to feel well and even write about them? But if humanity also meets any duty, and it must be added, it is a single operation that many duties must be performed. A letter is sent to your Most Illustrious Lordship concerning Theodore Rhaulis Issis, commending him to your Serenity, for which I have also entrusted some things to the most noble man Nicodemus to convey them to your Serenity. For the same reason I am writing now and commending him for the humanity of your lordship most solemnly. For it is both the work of piety and the clemency of your Serenity to help the poor, especially such as should either be brought up or live under royal protection. And not only because of many other things, but because of this also, your most serene Lordship will have me as an obliged and more constrained servant, whom I indeed wish to be always happy and blessed. From Florence on the 5th of September.

Your Lordship's most serene servant,

Jannis Argyropolus of Constantinople.

TO CARDINAL BESSARION

From Florence, Oct. 26 [?]

John Argyropolus to Cardinal Bessarion. He says health is the most important thing.

In my very bitter accident, and the miserable calamity of having lost two children within a few days in the very flower of youth, your divine work was offered to me against the approach of Plato's most faithful slanderers. And even though I was overwhelmed by the force of the calamity and the greatness of the pain, so that I could not control myself (for I could not resist the pain in any way), yet I read it at a time when my sometimes weary and exhausted nature was compelled to cease from mourning, and my mind was forced to be somewhat calm. In fact, I found in that work that I was sure that it could proceed from your acute intelligence and unique knowledge of all things. Surely nothing can be left out in that which seems to belong to the total perfection of the matter in question. In that there is an elegance of speech similar to the Platonic one; it is the subtlety and gravity of the sentences, it is the arrangement of things beyond which no other more convenient arrangement can be conceived and imagined. What more? It is the splendor of the book as a whole, that dignity, that artifice, which required both the intended materials and the dignity of the man whose parts were to be defended.

You did to Bessarion what seemed to be a learned man, what was just, what seemed to belong to the best manners, and you defended a most innocent, wisest man, the most meritorious of the human race, against unjust affections, and branded as ignorant and unscrupulous. Then you broke up the most absurd arguments of the story of him who had declared war against the divine man by some unknown plan. Besides, you have opened the opportunity not only to your parents, but also to your posterity, of the many excellent opinions of philosophers. For this reason, the mortal race owes you perpetual gratitude. But in the first place the Latins are subject to such a benefit to you. For after this, they will not be able to be seduced by initiatives of this kind, and they will accept those things which were seen by Aristotle to be grasped by Plato, and moreover they will think that Plato was such as nature knows about diseases. I cannot write more, and if the thing itself, in its greatness and dignity, it seems more glaring.

For the mind, oppressed by the greatness of pain, cannot properly perform any duty. Farewell, most holy man.

The 6th of November in Florence.

TO LORENZO MEDICI THE MAGNIFICENT

From Rome, Nov. 2, 1470

John Argyropylos, greetings to Lorenzo the Magnificent. From our second letter I have sent to you for the same cause and the same demands, and even if we appear to be troublesome to you, let us not be justly obliged in the matter of your friends and your excellent house: let us appear to be of so little importance that every trouble must be endured. I beseech you, therefore, most clearly to Laurence, that if that matter of ours is not yet complete, that you may give us some work for our relationship, that it may be speedily completed. We are deprived of our books, by an unjust fate beyond all hope, we are equally deprived of our translations, which are related to your most illustrious father Peter, and there are several eminent men and reverend fathers who are strongly affected to have them. Do not suffer, my Lorenzo, that we who have devoted ourselves to you and to your house may suffer the injury of some, perhaps through envy and avarice. We have always had you as our defender, the best of our patrons, in all our affairs; you have and will have; and with every breeze let us nourish true friends, not false ones: and your constant supporters of all. Farewell, and continue in your love for us, which we ourselves have perceived, and farewell again.

TO THE SAME

From Rome, Oct. 26, 1471

John Argyropylus to his great Lorenzo: health and perpetual happiness.

That which we obtained from you we have not yet attained. But if it is seen that it is to be obtained either by right or by grace, it is to be obtained from whom rather than from you. For thee and his most esteemed: Let him cease or let that enmity be broken to Codro: and be gracious to thy friends: and those who have merited merit from thee and thy elders: openly we never cease to preach. Wherefore we shall suffer it to be obtained from no other man, for several reasons. Not more. For I knew how to rejoice in short stories like that of James, and I was wont to add this to your praises. Good-bye, and let us post that now that you know that it is given by the statutes of your gymnasium, and that it was offered to us in writing and authorized by your father, the most famous man, and his colleagues when we were hired.

From the city on the 26th of October.

TO THE SAME

From Rome, Dec. 5, 1471

Johannes Argyopoulus to the Magnificent Lorenzo.

Thanks to you, my dear Laurence: we have recently received our goods without taking any revenue, and by your kindness you have entangled us all in the bush, and by no right, great or small, your humanity and kindness have never been unprepossessed to us. Now, having forgotten the notebooks which had been left there secretly, or rather in the notebook, I ordered them to be brought here. Moreover, I beseech you that they may not be hindered: order that they may be taken out without hindrance. From which the matter is great; I ask the more shamefully of you. But as easily as you can and are wont to be beneficial to us, so easily we ourselves ought not to neglect your benefits, without even waiting for them in return, and we can do them for you: understand that we are ready: for all things we may think to be of interest to you or to yours. We have no doubt that you are already convinced without our promise. Goodbye and love me as usual. From the city on the 8th of December.

TO THE SAME

From Rome, Apr. 3, 1472

John Argyropylus to Lorenzo the Magificent.

Your messenger is now going to the most illustrious leader. And when there is between him and you the highest affection and the highest love; and we shall return all ours to your most noble house: and you and yours. : by the innumerable favors bestowed on us by your ancestors and by you. We certainly desire nothing else; we desire nothing else, except that that prince and all the rest of the peoples and nations may perceive that we are yours as we are, and that we are devoted to your most noble and most illustrious family. Goodbye, always happy and blessed, and to us that you may always command yours for your honor and yours are always ready even to neglect life.

From the city on the 3rd of April.

TO THE DUKE OF MILAN

GALEAZZO MARIA SFORZA

From Rome, Apr. 3, 1472

To the Most Illustrious Prince GM Duke of Milan, Etc.

John Argyropylus Says the Most Salutation. And formerly your most noble virtues did not immoderately compel the princes to love you. For they are certainly not only to a man, but also to a prince, on whom depends the safety of many peoples, nations, and states; , we think ourselves to be the most ungrateful and most unjust.

We, therefore, do this for your duty to us, and with the courtesy that nothing should be considered greater. We offer you excellence, so much so that we even neglect life for your benefit. Farewell always, happy and happy conqueror, and take Isaac, the most loyal and respectful of your highness, as you have been accustomed to do with humanity, as your highness commanded, so I have done, and nothing will be more pleasing to me as a faithful middleman than to obey and serve him obediently to your excellency.

From the city on April 3, 1472.

TO LORENZO MEDICI THE MAGNIFICENT

From Rome, Feb. 11, 1476

John Argyropylus greetings to Lorenzo.

Antionius Rocca Pisanus, an excellent man and very familiar to me, obtained my letters to you by right friendship, by which I urged you to execute the rights of that murdered Peter Mastrani in order to preserve justice. I therefore exhort you, my sweetest Lorenzo, whom I am sure you will defend in justice, as in other human goods, to yield to no man of this storm, to do in this case also what you have always been accustomed to do in other cases. For what else is it fitting for you to do, or for me to remind you in this matter? You are a horse lover. I am a friend of both, and therefore I desire that their rights be preserved in your highest regard. If the father is aware of the murder, why should he not be punished for the murders as well? He must therefore be investigated by justice according to the law, and if he is found guilty, he must be judged liable to the crime. It certainly seems more probable that the son was driven to death by the authority of his father, if both of them, especially the father, pursued him with such hatred after he had been killed. But who would not assert that the father, as it was evident that he had done the matter in such a way, together with his son, had maliciously moved his hands towards the same, and had wrung the same beak for the same murder? Indeed, he was more of a murderer than his son, because of the reason of the first prince, his authority and deliberation, all men, if they were willing to confess the truth, would judge him with one word and one sentence. I would that you, my Lorenzo, should act in this matter in such a way that to all men the salvation of human society may be seen to be more with you than with the favor of some men. Goodbye, always be happy and love me as you always do.

Rome, the third of February.

TO LORENZO MEDICI THE MAGNIFICENT

From Rome, May 31, 1476

Jannes Argyropolus to his most magnificent Lorenzo the leap and eternal happiness.

With my books laid down, and my possessions in possession, I will go to you at the most pleasant opportunity, my Laurence. So, it's set where you like it. Goodbye half of my soul is always happy and blessed. Love from me as usual.

From the city, the day before the month of June.

LATIN TEXT

COMPENDIUM DE REGULIS ET FORMIS RATIOCINANDI PER IOHANNEM ARGYROPULUM EX OMNIBUS REGULIS BREVITER EXCERPTUM ATQUE COMPOSITUM GRATIA PHYLIPPI VALORRII DISCIPULI SUI

De Universalibus

Universalia seu predicabilia non transcendentia sunt quinque, Genus. Differentia, Species, Proprium et Accidens. Genus est id quod de pluribus differentibus specie hoc ipso quid est predicatur. Genus aliud est generalissimum, quod quidem tantum est genus, et nunquam est species; propterea quia supra se non habet aliud quid uti genus, ut substantia, qualitas et similia, aliud subalternum, quod quidem et genus et species est. Species ad superum, genus ad infera, ut animal, scienta et similia.

Species est id quod subicitur generi, uel quod de indiuiduis sine ullo medio predicatur. Species alia est specialissima: que quidem species tantum est, ut Homo, Equus. Albedo et quicquid est tale, alia subalterna, que quidem et species est et genus; perinde atque subalternum genus, ut animal scienta, color et quicquid est simile.

Differentia est id quo quippiam ab alio differt uel quo species genus execedit vel quod hoc ipso quale est in essentia, de quibus dicitur predicatur. Differentiae alie separabilis est, ut ambulatio, somnus et similia, alia insepararabilis est, ut ambulatio, somnus et similia, alia inseparabilis, cuis alia per accidens est, qualis est nigredo Ethiopis et albedo cerusae, alia per se, que quidem sola generum diusua est et specierum constitutiua, qua propter et specifica nuncupatur, ut rationale et irrationale; hominis illud, hoc beluae talis est differentia.

Proprium est id quod alicui universali consistit uel per se accidit. Proprium aliud alicui quidem uti dictum est soli accidit, non tamen cullibet competit eorum quae sunt sub illo, quale est mederi, respectu hominis, citharamque pulsare. Aliud alicui quidem accidit et cullibet eorum competit, que sub illo sunt collocata. Non tamen illi accidit soli, ut bipes ac quadrupes. Illud enim homini, hoc leoni competit: hoc modo proprium est. Aliud et soli accidit tali atque omnibus quidem competit, quae sunt sub illo et semper etiam competit risibile hoc modo hominis et rugibile leonis proprium est. Hoc et proprie proprium dicitur et mutuam cum eo cui competit suscipit predicatiinem. Quicquid enim est homo risibile est et quicquid est risibile homo est.

Accidents est id quod adesse et abesse potest sine subiecti corruptione et quod eidem inesse potest et non inesse. Hoc duplex est. Aliud enim est separabile, ut somnus, ambulatio et similia, aliud inseparabile, ut albedo respectu cerusae et nigredo respectu corui et Ethiopis atque picis. Id libere cogitatione abesse potest sine subiecti corruptione.

De Predicamentis

Predicamentum est inter conceptus ordo superos inferosque quo superi predicati inferi subiecti natura subeunt roborem. Predicamenta in quibis sunt ea quae diximus predicabilia decem sunt, substantia, qualitas, qualititas, ad aliquem seu relatio, ubi, quando, habere, situm esse, agere, pati. Ad Quae sane conseptus omnis haud transcendens reducitur substantia, ut homo, bos, equus; quantitas, ut numerus, linea, superficies, qualitas, ut caliditas, albedo, dulcedo, amaritudo; relatio, ut paternitas, filioatio, similitudo ac dissimilitudo: ubi, ut in foro, in templo, Florentiae, Romae; quando, ut hodie, cras, kalendis, nonis, idibus et quicquid his simile; habere, ut indutum esse, armatum et id genus; situm esse, ut iacere, stare atque sedere; agere, ut incidere, urere, pungere, atque unicere; pati, ut incidi, uri, pungi et uinci. Atque cum per se quidem horum singula concipiuntur aut dicuntur, nulla prorsus inde sit aut affirmatio aut negatio; cum autem inter sese connectuntur, affirmatio continue pululat aut negatio.

De Substantia

Substantiae alia est corpus, alia corpis expers; corpus aliud est animatum, aliud inanimatum; animatum aliud est sensitiuum, aliud non sensitiuum; sensitiuum quod quidem est animal, aliud particepts, aliud expers est rationis; particeps roboris, aliud mortale, aliud immortale est. Illic est homo sub quo sunt singuli homines, ut Cicero, Scipio, Plato, hic celum, sub quo tamque specie celum hoc est et partes ipsius rationes similes subeuntes. Expers autem rationis belua est, sub qua per differntias diversas species multorum animalium singule, collocantur, ut et homo, sub quibus singulis individua collocantur solo numero differntia, sub equo hic equus et ille, sub boue his bos et ille et eodem in ceteris modo. Pari modo et ipsum non sensituum dividendum est quod quidem platam esse constat, quae per differntiam in herbam, fruticem arboremque diffunditur; atque herba quidem ueluti genus in uarias species, in maluam, marubium, veratrum ceteraque talia diuidatur. Gued si haec sunt spetialissiem species, sub ipsis singularia collocantur, sub malua haec et illa, sub marubio hoc et illud, et eodem de ceteris modo. Frutex autem in rubum, rosam et tales species per differentias divifatur quod si eae specialissime sunt, sub ipsos individua continuo collocantur, sub rubo hec et illa, sub rose hec et illa, et simile de ceteris modo. Arbos etiam uti genus et ipsa suas in species per differentias diffunditur, in nucem, ficum, oliuam, pinum, abietem, ceteraque similias genus, sub quibussi specialiisima sunt, individua sunt continuo collacanda, haec nux et illa sub nuce, haec ficus et illa sub ficu et de ceteris modo eodem. Eadem et in on animato agenda sunt. Dividendum enim et ipsum ut genus per differentias suas in species est, in elementa, in quibus ignem, aerem, aquam, tteram et ea quae ex elementis constant: expertia vite qualia sunt minerabilia ipse, lapides, in quibus stagnum, argentum, aurum, alumen, sulphur: id genus et quicquid inter haec cadit et elementa. Denique de corporis experte substantia persimilis est per omnia ratio. Secanda enim per differentias ut genus et illa suas in species dividatur. Has separatas substantias esse constat, quas et mentes et intelligentias appelare solemus, in quibuset in unaquaque specie individuum unum perpetuum est. Excipiatur deus gloriosus, qui quidem illimitatus est ac infinitus et hoc pacto plenius praedicamentum substantiae dividi potest. Aristoteles autem hoc modo distribuisse ipsum videtur. Substantiam non aliam primam esse dicit, aliam secundum per primam quoduis individuum; per secundum species generaque intelligendo; atque illud quidem primo et propriissimam atque maximam substantias asserit esse. Species autem et genera non ita substantias esse quam que species, magis substantias quam genera dicit esse.

Competiti omni substantie in subiecto non esse et si non soli, nam et differentie substantia competit. Competit prime substantiae hoc, aliquid significare: competit etiam omni substantiae ut nihil ipse contrarium sit et ut non suscipiat in se per latitudem gradus magisque ac minus substantia sit. Maxime tamen substantie properium esse videtur unum idemque ipsam persistere suique mutatione susceptiuum esse contrariorum. Et haec sint satis de substania dicta.

25

Pros Nicodemon Tragkedinan
Ex Phlorentias, 1 Aug. 1460

Johannes Argiropilus Constantinopilanus Nicodemo nobilissimo et preclarissimo viro, domino Nicodemo serenissimi ducis Mediolani egregio oratori, suo patri percolendo salutem.

Non sensi tuum recessum. Nam si sensissem et tuam prestanciam rogassem ut illam rem peregas, et ad serenisimum principem litteras dedissem. Nunc tandem sensi et statim ad prestabilitatem tuam has exaravi et ad serenissimum litteras dedi. Obsecro igtur tuam humanitatem, ut rem illam dilligentius agas, ut des meas litteras serenissimo et ut me sue serenitati vehementer commendes. Sum enim eius servus fidelis atque perpetuus. Vale vir prestantissime et me ama. Ex Florentia 1 Aug. 1460.

Puer de quo diximus Theodorus appellatur Rhaul et est filius nobilis viri Nicholai Rhaulis.

Nobilissime atque magnifice vir. Vidi atque percepi ea que ad me vestra nobilitas scripsit, et etiam que percepit clarissimus et disertissimus vir Filelfus. Et cum non habeam domi librum Plitarchi illum dabo operam ut paulo post habeam illum et videam illum passum quo pacto se se habet; deinde ad vestram prestabilitatem scribam.

Pros ton Auton
Ex Florentias, 5 Sept. 1460

Johannes Agiropulus Constantinopolitanus nobilissimo et preclarissimo viro domino Nicodemo suo aimico percolendo salutem.

Et paulo ante litteras ad nobilitatam tuam dedi una cum litteras quas ad illum dedi, et nunc etiam identidem facio. Rogo itaque ut has etiam litteras des serenissimo principi et me ei plurimum commendes et etiam illum puerum de quo nobilitati tue nonnulla locutus sum, qui quidem sub tutella illustrissimi principis vivit THeodorusque appellatur Rhaul, filius nobilis viri greci domini Nicolai Rhaulis Issis. Quod si illud quod nobilitati tue dixi fuerit impetratum, litteris antea certiorem me redde. Sin minus fiet, at id tamen nobilitatem tuam summopere rogo ut puerum iam dictum plurimum serenissimo principi mea ex parte commendes. Hoc cum cetereis officium magis obligatum me tue nobilitati redder. Vale felix et fac ut a serenissimo principe litteras habeamus pro ijs que scripsimus ut auctoritatis aliquid te intercedente apud allum consequamur. Vale iterum felix et me ut soles ama. Ex Florentia V die septembris 1460.

Pros Ton Douka Mediolanou
Fragkiskon Sfortsan
Ex Florentias, 5 Sept. 1468

Illustrissime et Serenissime Princeps. Paulo ante litteras ad Illustrissimam Dominationem tuam per nobilissimum Virum Nocidemum dedi. Et nunc etiam scribo. Quod quidem non importuni hominis ut puto, sed obbligati vehementer videbitur. Quid enim aliud benivolos servos absentes erga suos dominos agere decet, quam et bene de illis sentire et etiam scribere? Quod si humanitatis etiam quippiam occurrat officium et illud addendum est, est una operatione plura officia sunt exercenda. Scripso igitur ad Illustrissimam Dominationem tuam de Theodoro Rhaulis Issis, commendando illum serenitati tu pro qua etiam nonnulla nobilissimo viro Nicodemo imposui ut ea Serenitati referat tuae. Pro eodem etiam et nunc scribo et ipsum humanitati summe sereissime dominationis tue commendo. Est enim et pietatis opus et clementie Serenitatis tue succurrere miseris, presertim talibus quod sub regia tutella vel educari vel vivere decet. Atque me non solum propter cetera multa, set ob hoc etiam obligatum magisque obstrictum servum habebit perpetuo serenissima Dominatio tua, quam quidem exopto felicem esse semper atque beatam. Ex Florentia V die Septembris.

Serenissime Dominationis tue.

Servus Iannis Argyropulus Constantinopolitanus.

Pros Ton Kardinalion Bessariona
Ex Florentias, Oct. 26 [?]

Ioannes Argyropylus Bessarioni cardinali. Salutem plurimam dicit.

In ipso meo acerbissimo casu ac miserabili calamitate duobus liberis intra paucas dies in ipso flore iuventutis amissis, diuinum opus tuum mihi oblatum est adversus Platonis nostri fedissimum calumniatorum aditum. Quod et si vi calamitatis et doloris magnitudine opprimebas ut mei compos esse non possem (nullem enim modo resistere dolori poteram) perlegi tamen eo tempore quo fessa aliquando ac defatigata natura cessare a luctu et animus aliquanto tranquillus esse cogebatur. Ea vero in eo opere inveni quae ab acutissimo tuo ingenio et singulari rerum omnium scientia proficisci posse certo sciebam. Nihil profecto desierati in eo potest quod ad summam rei de qua agitur perfectionem pertinere videatur. Est in illo elegantia sermonis platonice similis; est subtilitas gravitasque sententiarum, est preterea dispositio rerum qua nulla alia acoomodatior excogitari fingique potest. Quid plura? Est splendor libri totius, ea dignitas, id artificium, quae et proposita materies et eius viri cuius partes difendebantur dignitas postulabat.

Egisti Bessario quod ad eruditum virum, quod ad iustum, quod ad optimos mores pertinere videbatur, et hominem innocentissimum, sapientissimum, optime de hominum genere meritum contumeliis affectum iniquis et ut ignarum et flagitiosum notatum defendisti. Tum fabulae illius qui divino homini bellum nescio quo consilio indixerate rationes ineptissimas dissoluisti. Preterea multas praeclarasque sententias philosophorum occasionem nactus non modo parentibus set etiam posteris aperuisti. Qua propter non mediocres tibi perpetuo gratias genus mortalium debet. In primis autem tanti tibi benefitii obnoxii sunt Latini. Neque enim post hac hujusmodi inceptiis seduci poterunt et ea quibus ab Aristotele carpi Plato videretur ita ut capienda sunt accipient et Platonem insuper talem fuisse qualis natura morbibus scienta uit, si auctoritati doctorum hominum credere, si rationibus obtemperare valuerint existimabunt. Plura scribere nequeo et si res ipsa, magnitudine dignitateque sua, plura efflagirate videtur.

Mens enim magnitudine doloris oppressa nullum recte exercere offictium potest. Vale vir santissime.

Florentiae VI calendas novembris

Pros Laurention Medikon ton Megaloapeiia
Ex Romas, 2 Nov. 1470

Ioannes Argyropylos Magnifico Laurentio suo salutem. Eces secunde littere nostre eadem de causa eademque postulantes ad te misse sunt atque et si molesti tibi esse videamur: ne tamen iusta in re tui amici tueque preclare domui obligati: tam parui pensi esse videamur omnis molestia est subeunda. Obsecro igitur te, preclarissime Laurenti ut, si res illa nostra nondum est absoluta: detur abs te opera pro nostra necessitudine: ut cito perficiatur. Libris nostris, iniquo fato summa sum iniuria preter spem omnem caremus, traductionibus nostris, que ad preclarissimum patrem tuum Petrum referuntur pari modo caremus, et sunt complures prestantissimi viri reverndique patres qui illas habere vehementer affectant. Noli pati, mi Laurenti: ut nos tibi dediti domuique tue, ob invidiam fortasse ac avariciam nonnullorum iniuriam patiamur. Te defensorem, te patronum optimum, omnibus in nostris rebus semper habuimus, te esse et hanc rem instantem: et omnes futuras referimus habuisti nos; habes atque habebis; quouque aura uescamur amicos veros, non fictos: et tuos tuorumque omnium perpetuos fautores. Vale et in tuo amore erga nos que re ipse percepimus persevera atque iterum vale Ex urbe, ii novembris.

Pros Ton Auton
Ex Romas, 26 Oct. 1471

Joannes Argyropylus Laurentio suo magnifico: salutem perpetuamque foelicitatem.

Illud quod abs te impetrauimus: nondum assequuti sumus. Quod si aut iure aut gratia consequendum esse uidetur: a quonam queso potius quam abs te est impetrandum. Te enim et eiuem uistissimum: Iiuor cesset: aut inuidia rumpantur ilia Codro: et gratum erga tuos amicos: quique de te tuisque maioribus benemeriti sunt: aperte nunquam desistimus predicare. Quare illud a nullo alio homine compluribus de causis equo animo consequi patiemur. Non plura. Ie enim ut Iaconem gaudere perbreuibus noui: atque hoc addere tuis laudibus consueui. Vale et nos id postere nunc scias quod a statutis uestri gymnasii datur et quod a patre tuo uiro clarissimo suisque collegis cum conducebamur oblatum est nobis scripto atque pormissum.

Ex Urbe XXVI octobris.
Ex Romas, 5 Dec. 1471

Johannes Argyopylus Magnificentissimo Laurentio suo.
Benefitio tuo mi Laurenti: res nostra nuper accepimus sine sumpti ullo uectigalium tuaque benignitate omnibus in rubus smper nos conplexus es, nec ullo iure sive magno sive paruo tua humanitas benignitasque nunquam nobis non preseto fuit. Nunc obliuione libelli qui clam uel potius scartabelli relicti istic sunt, eos huc afferi iussi. Ceterum ne impediantur te precor: iubeas ut sine impedimento extrahi liceat. Quominus res est magna; eo uerecundius a te peto. Sed quam facile tu potes et soles in nos esse beneficus tam facile ipsi debemus tua beneficia non negligere quin etiam expetere ultro et tibi pro ys possumus: paratos nos esse intelligas: ad omnia uidelicet que aut tua aut tuorum interesse putemus. Quod iam sine nostra pollicitatione persuasum tibi esse non dubitamus. Vale et me ut soles ama. Ex urbe vii decmrbis.

Pros Ton Auton
Ex Romas, 3 Apr. 1472

Iohannes Argyropylus Magnificio Laurentio. Salutem.
Isatius tuus ad illustrissimum ducem nunc proficiscitur. Atque cum sit inter illum et te summa beniuolentia summusque amor; et nos omnia nostra ad tuam nobilissimam domum: et te tuosque referamus: rogo et obsecro ut litteris tuis ipsum Isatium illustrissimo illi principi comendes, non comendatione quadam uulgari: Set ea qua princeps ille nos tuos penitus esse cognoscar: tueque domui preclarissime deditos addatur et hos: beneficiis sine numero illis que a maioribus tuis atque abs te in nos liberalissime sunt collata. Nihil aliud nos profecto expetimus, nihil aliud affectamus: nisi ut ille princeps cetereque omnes gentes et nationes nos tuos esse ut sumus: et tuo generi nobilissimo preclarissimeque tue domui deditos omino percipiant. Vale perpetuo felix atque beatus et nobis ut tuis semper mandare uelis pro honor tuo tuorumque semper paratis etiam negligere uitam.
Ex urbe iii aprilis.

Pros Ton Douka Mediolanos
Galeatson Marian Sfortsan
Ex Romas, 3 Apr. 1472

Illustrissimo Principi G.M. Duci Mediolanensi, Etc.

Ioannes Argyropylus Salutem Plurimam Dicit. Et antea nobilissime tuaw virtutes Illme Princepsnos ad te diligendum non mediocriter compellebant. Sunt enim profecto non solum ad hominem sed ad principem etiam accomodatissime, a quo multaram gentium nationum civitatumque salus dependet, et nun tue ad nos littere omni humanitate officioque referte adeo nos ad te amandum colendumve compulerent ut si te summa beniuolentia semper, summoque amore non prosequamur, nos ipsos ingratissimos ac iniquissimos esse putemus.

Nos itaque pro tuo erga nos officio atque humanitate quo nihil maius esse existimanus ide agimus, nos ipsos. Ecellantie tue offerimus atque adeo ut pro quovis tuo commodo vitam etiam negligamus. Vale semper victor foelix atque beatus, et Isaccium tue celsitudini deditissimum atque observantissimum ut consuevisti facere cum humanirate suscipe ut iussit Celsitudo tua ita feci, necque medius fidius mihi iocundius quicquam erit quam hunc Ecellentie tue obtemperate obsequi atque servire. Ex Urbe iii Aprilis 1472.

Pros Laurention Medikon Megaloprepa
Ex Romas, 11 Feb. 1476

Ioannes Argyropylus Laurentio suo salutem.
Antionius Rocca Pisanus, vir egregius et mihi familiarissimus, meas ad te litteras iure amicitie impetravit, quibus te ad iusticiam servandam interfaecti illius Petri Mastrani iura exequenda hortarer. Hortor itaque te, mi suavissime Laurenti, quem ut in ceteris bonis humanis, sic et in iusticia defenda nemini tempestatis huiusce homini cedere certo scio, ut hac etiam in causa id aga quod et in ceteris agere semper consuevisti. Quid enim aliud aut te facere, aut me te admonere hac in causa dece? Tu es equitatis amator. Ego sum utriusque amicus, atque ideo iura ilius tuo maxime munere servari percupio. Si pater homicide conscius est cedis, cur non et homicidia et ipse lueret penas? Illud igitur inquiratur iusticie lege, consciusque si fuerit inventus, obnoxius crimini iudicetur. PLusquam verisimile profecto esse videtur compulsi patris auctoritateque filium decem egrisse, si uterque, magisque pater, interfectum illum odio tanto persequebatur. At eum patreum, quam ita rem gesisse constaret, quis non asseruerit una cum filio et manus ad idem scelusmovisse, et mucronem eundem ad eandem necem strincisse? Illum magis homicidam profecto quam filius, ratione sane primi princippi, auctoramenti deliberationisque, omnes homines,

si vera fateri velint, uno ore unaque sententia iudicarent. Tu, mi, Laurenti, hac in causa ita agas velim, ut ad universsi hominibus plus apud te societatis humane salus quam nonnullorum hominum valere gratia videatur. Vale perpetuo felix et me, ut soles, ama. Raptim.
Rome, terio idus februarii.

Pros Laurention Medikon Ton Megalo
Ex Romas, 31 Mai 1476

Jaanes Argyropylus magnificentissimo Laurentio suo saltum perpetuamque felicitatem.

Libris depositis: habitisque pecuiniis: ad te iocundissime mi Laurenti sumpta oportunitate proficiscar. Ita est statutum ubi tibi placet. Vale dimidium animi mei perpetuo felix atque beatus. Ex me ut soles ama.
Ex urbe, pridie Kalendis Juniis.

The Scriptorium Project is the work of a small group of lay people of various apostolic churches who are interested in the preservation, transmission, and translation of the works of the early and medieval church. Our efforts are to make the works of the church fathers accessible to anyone who might have an interest in Christian antiquities and the theological, philosophical, and moral writings that have become the bedrock of Western Civilization.

To-date, our releases have pulled from the Greek, Syriac, Georgian, Latin, Armenian, Indo-Persian, Germanic, Nordic, Slavic, Celtic, Ethiopian, and Coptic traditions of Christianity, and have been pulled from sundry local traditions and languages.

Other Selections from the Byzantine Church Series:

Catholic Council of Fourth Constantinople by Basil I, Eastern Roman Emperor (Dec. 2006)
Funeral Oration for Bessarion by Michael Apostolius (Mar. 2007)
Treatise on Sobriety by Nicephorus the Solitary (Apr. 2007)
Select Acts by John Bessarion (Oct. 2008)
Defense of the orthodox Catholic Doctrines of the Latins by John Bessarion (Mar. 2009)
Sermons by Nestorius of Constantinople (May 2009)
Orthodox Council of Fourth Constantinople by Photius of Constantinople (Dec. 2009)
On the Death of Manuel II by John Bessarion (June 2010)
Theophrastus by Aeneas of Gaza (Apr. 2011)
Treatise on Prayer by St. Evargius of Ponticus (May 2011)
The Lausiac History by St. Palladius of Galatia (Mar. 2013)
Letter on the Fall of Constantinople by Isidore of Kiev (Oct. 2013)
The Hesychast by Gregory of Sinai (June 2015)
Selected Laws by Justinian I, Emperor of Rome (July 2018)
Exhortation to Monks Ordained in India by St. John of Karpathos (March 2021)
Fragments of 'Chronicle' by Hippolytus of Thebes (May 2023)
The Life of the Blessed Theotokos by Epiphanius Monachus (July 2023)
Letters of Nestorius by Nestorius of Constantinople (Sept. 2023)
Eleven Letters & Other Writings by John Argyropoulos (May 2024)

www.ingramcontent.com/pod-product-compliance
Lightning Source LLC
LaVergne TN
LVHW052049070526
838201LV00086B/5159